THIS BOOK BELONGS TO

_____

_____

REFLECTIONS
— ON —
ENGLAND

Green fields of England! whereso'er
Across this watery waste we fare,
One image at our hearts we bear,
Green fields of England, everywhere.
ARTHUR HUGH CLOUGH

The solid mountains were as bright as clouds
Grain-tinctured, drench'd in empyrean light
WILLIAM WORDSWORTH

There will we sit upon the rocks,
And see the shepherds feed their flocks
By shallow rivers, to whose falls
Melodious birds sing madrigals.
CHRISTOPHER MARLOWE

A crisp January day in
Great Langdale, Cumbria.

These English. They love their old ways yet, and
their old masters, and their old land.
JOHN RUSKIN

❀

Forget six counties overhung with smoke,
Forget the snorting steam and piston stroke,
Forget the spreading of the hideous town,
Think rather of the pack-horse on the down,
And dream of London, small and white and clean,
And clear Thames bordered by its gardens green.
WILLIAM MORRIS

❀

And through the coloured medieval pages
The old road runs like script, with glittering scenes
Of pomp, and pageantry, and pilgrimages –
Merchants and friars, knights and kings and queens:
A cavalcade of England in the blending,
Of fighting factions lost, and freedom won;
While wayside hermits bridge and path are mending,
That to God's house the road may still go on.
C.W. SCOTT-GILES

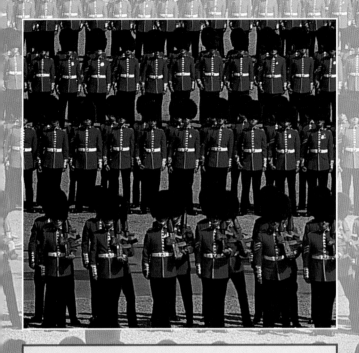

Had I had an English army I could
have conquered the universe.
NAPOLEAN BONAPARTE

*Trooping the colour on Horseguards Parade, in
honour of the Official Birthday of H.M. The Queen.*

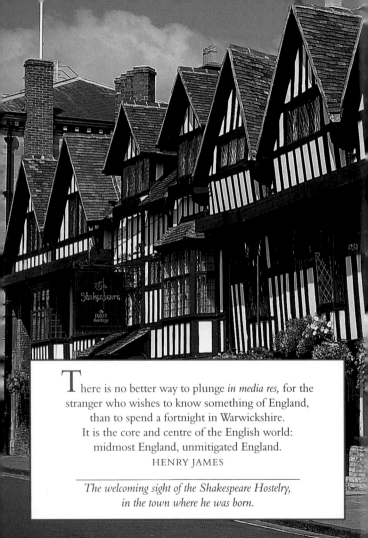

There is no better way to plunge *in media res,* for the stranger who wishes to know something of England, than to spend a fortnight in Warwickshire. It is the core and centre of the English world: midmost England, unmitigated England.

HENRY JAMES

The welcoming sight of the Shakespeare Hostelry, in the town where he was born.

Is there a corner of land, a furze-fringed rag of a by-way,
    Coign of your foam-white cliffs or swirl of your
                    grass-green waves,
            Leaf of your peaceful copse,
            or dust of your strenuous highway,
But in our hearts is sacred, dear as our cradle, our graves?
                    E. NESBIT

Rolling home, rolling home,
    Rolling home across the sea,
Rolling home to merry England,
Rolling home dear land to thee.
TRADITIONAL SEA SHANTY

Others may use the ocean as their road,
Only the English make it their abode.
            EDMUND WALLER

The tumbling cliffs at Lands End,
England's most westerly point.

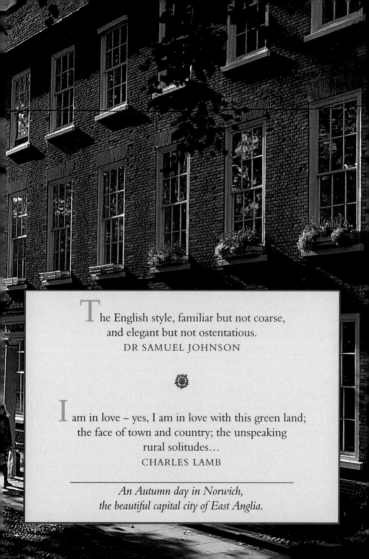

The English style, familiar but not coarse,
and elegant but not ostentatious.
DR SAMUEL JOHNSON

❧

I am in love – yes, I am in love with this green land;
the face of town and country; the unspeaking
rural solitudes…
CHARLES LAMB

An Autumn day in Norwich,
the beautiful capital city of East Anglia.

Woods, fields, brooks
Are life eternal – and in silence they
Speak happiness – beyond the reach of books.
JOHN CLARE

I think that I shall never see,
A poem lovely as a tree.
JOYCE KILMER

Under the greenwood tree,
Who loves to lie with me,
And tune his merry throat
Unto the sweet bird's note,
Come hither, come hither, come hither!
Here shall he see,
No enemy
But winter and rough weather.
WILLIAM SHAKESPEARE

*A fallow deer grazes amid the bracken in
Ashdown Forest, East Sussex.*

All that a man might ask thou hast given me, England,
  Birthright and happy childhood's long heartsease,
And love whose range is deep beyond all sounding,
        And wider than all seas:
    A heart to front the world and find God in it,
    Eyes blind enough but not too blind to see
  The lovely things behind the dross and darkness,
        And lovelier things to be.
                R.E.VERNEDE

God! I will pack, and take a train,
And get me to England once again!
For England's the one land, I know,
Where men with splendid hearts may go.

RUPERT BROOKE

The elegant front of Polesden Lacey, Surrey,
now in the care of The National Trust.

England – not like other countries,
but all a planted garden.
DANIEL DEFOE

Such little hills, the sky
Can stoop to tenderly and the wheat-fields climb;
Such nooks of valleys lined with orchises,
Fed full of noises by invisible streams…
ELIZABETH BARRETT BROWNING

England is very small and very green
And full of little lanes all dense with flowers
That wind along and lose themselves between
Mossed farms and parks and fields of quiet sheep.
And in the hamlets where her stalwarts sleep
Low bells chime out from old elm-hidden towers.
GEOFFREY HOWARD

England Home, and Beauty!
CHARLES DICKENS

I would rather sleep in the southern corner
of a little English chuchyard than in the tomb
of all the Capulets.
EDMUND BURKE

*Poppies – the crowning glory
of the English meadows.*

Life is good, and joy runs high
Between English earth and sky.
WILLIAM ERNEST HENLEY

A pulse in the eternal mind, no less
Gives somewhere back the thoughts by England given
Her sights and sounds, dreams happy as her day;
And laughter learnt of friends; and gentleness,
In hearts at peace, under an English heaven.
RUPERT BROOKE

And the May month flaps
its glad green leaves like wings.
THOMAS HARDY

Sir, we are a nest of singing birds.
DR SAMUEL JOHNSON

*Morris men dancing in the High Street
at Framlingham in Suffolk.*

The poorest man may in his cottage bid defiance to all the force of the Crown. It may be frail; its roof may shake; the wind may blow through it; the storms may enter. But the King of England cannot enter; all his forces dare not cross the threshold of the ruined tenement.

WILLIAM PITT

The charm of England is the vast variety of scenery, atmosphere, everything in small spaces.

GEORGE GISSING

And for a minute a blackbird sang
Close by, and round him, mistier,
Farther and farther, all the birds
Of Oxfordshire and Gloucestershire.

EDWARD THOMAS

*Arlington Row in Bibury,
one of the gems of the Cotswolds.*

The sky to the north was of a chastened yet rich yellow, fading into pale blue, and streaked and scattered over with steady islands of purple, melting away into shades of pink. It was like a vision to me …

DOROTHY WORDSWORTH

H ow lovely is a summer's eve
That's full of heavenly light …
WILLIAM H. DAVIES

Dusk falls on the beautiful city of Bath.

Coombe and tor, green meadow and lane,
Birds on the waving bough,
Beetling cliffs by the surging main,
Rich red loam for the plough;
Devon's the fount of the bravest blood
That braces England's breed,
Her maidens fair as the apple-pie bud,
And her men are men in deed.
HAROLD BOULTON

Where are the Yeomen, the Yeomen of England?
In homestead and in cottage they still dwell in England!
Stained with the ruddy tan,
God's air doth give a man,
Free as the winds that fan the broad breast of England!
BASIL HOOD

England may be a small country, but no country
in the world has such diversity of soils, climates,
natural resources and topography in such small space.
W.G.HOSKINS

*A bright summer's day at Torquay harbour,
on Devon's south coast.*

There bursts upon your view, with all its towers, forests and streams… an ancient city, or a fair castle rising out of the forests.

SYDNEY SMITH

There was a man once loved green fields like you,
He drew his knowledge from the wild bird's songs,
And he had praise for every beauteous thing,
And he had pity for all piteous wrongs…

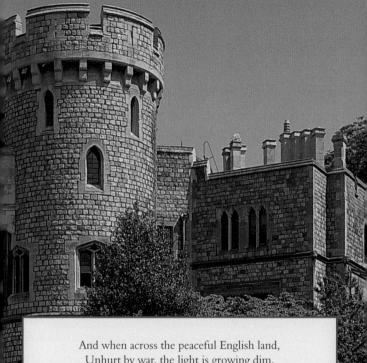

And when across the peaceful English land,
Unhurt by war, the light is growing dim,
And you remember by your shadowed bed
All those – the brave – you must remember him,
And know it was for you to bear his name
And such as you that all his joy he gave,
His love of quiet fields, his youth, his life,
To win that heritage of peace you have.

MARJORIE WILSON

The Norman Gate, Windsor Castle.

Oh how I love, on a fair summer's eve,
When streams of light pour down the golden west ...
JOHN KEATS

On this kindly yellow day
of mild low-travelling winter sun
The stirless depths of the yews
Are vague with misty blues:
Across the spacious pathway
stretching spires of shadow run,
And the wind-gnawed walls of ancient brick
are fired vermillion.
THOMAS HARDY

He loved birds, and green places, and the wind upon
the heath, and saw the brightness of the skirts of God.
GRAVESTONE INSCRIPTION OF NATURALIST
W.H.HUDSON

Morcott Mill in Leicestershire,
at the close of the day.

Soft as a cloud is yon blue Ridge –
the Mere Seems firm as solid crystal, breathless,
clear, and motionless.
WILLIAM WORDSWORTH

❧

If I was a young English painter, I would spend all
my time painting the English countryside.
PABLO PICASSO

❧

Grasmere looked so beautiful that my heart
was almost melted away.
It was quite calm, only spotted with sparkles of light.
DOROTHY WORDSWORTH

❧

A corner of England's Lake District:
Blea Tarn below Side Pike.

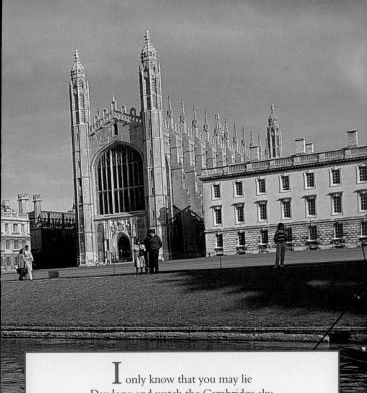

I only know that you may lie
Day long and watch the Cambridge sky,
And, flower-lulled in sleepy grass,
Hear the cool lapse of hours pass…

RUPERT BROOKE

Punting past King's College Chapel and
Clare College on the River Cam at Cambridge.

Clear had the day been from the dawn,
  All chequer'd was the sky,
Thin clouds, like scarfs of cobweb lawn,
  Veil'd Heaven's most glorious eye.
MICHAEL DRAYTON

*The proud ruins of Dunstanburgh Castle,
on the bleak Northumberland coast.*

And did those feet, in ancient time
Walk upon England's mountains green?
And was the Holy lamb of God
On England's pleasant pastures seen?

WILLIAM BLAKE

England – a happy land we know,
Where follies naturally grow.

CHARLES CHURCHILL

Merrily, merrily, shall I live now,
Under the blossom that hangs on the bough.
WILLIAM SHAKESPEARE

Loveliest of trees, the cherry now
Is hung with bloom along the bough,
And stands about the woodland ride
Wearing white for Eastertide.
A.E. HOUSMAN

*Blossom time at Anne Hathaway's cottage,
in Shakespeare's Stratford-upon-Avon.*

Happy is England! I could be content
To see no other verdure than its own;
To feel no other breezes than are blown
Through its tall woods with high romances blent.
JOHN KEATS

The English winter, ending in July,
To recommence in August.
LORD BYRON

His daily teachers had been woods and rills,
The silence that is in the starry sky,
The sleep that is among the lonely hills.
WILLIAM WORDSWORTH

*Winter mists at Westonbirt Arboretum
in Gloucestershire.*

So will I build my altar in the fields,
And the blue sky my fretted dome shall be.
SAMUEL TAYLOR COLERIDGE

*York Minster, seen from the city walls
on a clear summer's day.*

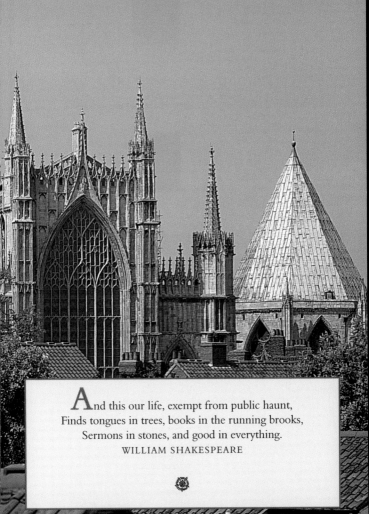

And this our life, exempt from public haunt,
Finds tongues in trees, books in the running brooks,
Sermons in stones, and good in everything.
WILLIAM SHAKESPEARE

ALSO IN THIS SERIES

Reflections on Scotland

First published in Great Britain in 1998 by
JARROLD PUBLISHING LTD
Whitefriars, Norwich NR3 1TR

Developed and produced by
FOUR SEASONS PUBLISHING LTD
London, England

Text research by *Tom King*
Designed and typeset by *Judith Pedersen*
Printed in Dubai

ISBN 0 7117 0986 6

ACKNOWLEDGEMENTS

Four Seasons Publishing Ltd would like to thank all those
who kindly gave permission to reproduce the words and visual
material in this book; copyright holders have been identified where
possible and we apologise for any inadvertent omissions.

Front Cover: *Poppies* Copyright © RICHARD TILBROOK
Back Cover: *Morris men* CHARLES J.NICHOLAS
Title Page: *Warwick Castle* NEIL JINKERSON
Endpapers: *Rydal Water* CHARLES J.NICHOLAS

Other photographs by: DENNIS AVON, ALAN BARNES, J.A. BROOKS,
NEIL JINKERSON, ANDREW MORRIS, CHARLES J. NICHOLAS,
ANDREW PERKINS, ROY RAINFORD, P. STRONG,
RICHARD TILBROOK, PAUL THOMPSON.

All photographs copyright of *Jarrold Publishing Ltd.*
unless otherwise indicated.